DATE DUE

AP 16 '15			

This Book Donated by

IRELAND

IRELAND
YOUR ONLY PLACE

Jan Morris & Paul Wakefield

Clarkson N. Potter, Inc./Publishers

Published by Clarkson N. Potter, Inc., 201 East 50th Street, New York, New York 10022

Originally published in Great Britain by Aurum Press Limited in 1990

CLARKSON N. POTTER, POTTER, and colophon are trademarks of Clarkson N. Potter, Inc.

Designed by Philip Mann/Ace Ltd   Manufactured in Italy

Front jacket photograph: Ballynakill, County Galway
Back jacket photograph: Sheila O'Shea, Sneem, County Kerry

The extract on page 156 is taken from *At Swim-Two-Birds* by Flann O'Brien (copyright 1951, 1966 by Brian Nolan). Reprinted by kind permission of Grafton Books, a division of William Collins and Sons Ltd, and of Walker and Company.

Library of Congress Cataloging-in-Publication Data
Morris, Jan, 1926–
Ireland: your only place/text by Jan Morris: photographs by Paul Wakefield.
            p.   cm. $30.00
1. Ireland—Description and travel—1981– 2. Morris, Jan, 1926– —Journeys—Ireland. I. Title.
DA978.2.M67 1990
914.1504′824—dc20   89–49555

ISBN 0-517-58005-5
10 9 8 7 6 5 4 3 2 1
First American Edition

1 THE VIEW FROM THE PINNACLE

On a small stubbly hill at Glassan north of Athlone, close to the farm where Mr and Mrs John Nally have brought up their seven sons, a venerable stone pinnacle is said to mark the geographical centre of Ireland, at 53°.30′N, 7°.50′W. This is more or less on a level with Slutsk in the Pripet Marshes, Lake Atikonak in Labrador or the northernmost tip of China, parallels I choose in order to emphasize from the start that no references can be too far-fetched for Ireland. So close across the sea from my home in Wales that on clear days we can see it on our western horizon, the country has tantalized me always with its hazed allure, and made me feel that no Slutsk or Arctic mere could be more exotic.

However, I intended at first to give this essay about the country some measure of rational control, so I started my work by making straight for the Glassan Pinnacle, hoping to find in it an opening figure of Ireland that was positive, graspable and ordered. Perhaps if I touched it, I mocked myself, as one kisses a holy relic, I would be revealed some instantly logical vision of the island. I had to scramble over a ramshackle dry-stone wall to reach the monument, beyond the Nallys' outbuildings with their tractor and three Japanese cars, and found that while it was a fairly unlovely thing in itself, it did command a most reassuring view. The day was fine, the sky was splendid, rooks cawed above my head, and as far as I could see benign pasture-lands extended over unassuming hills, ornamented here and there with mansions.

The district stood, I happened to know from a recent survey in the *Irish Times*, very low on the scale of Ireland's upward social mobility, meaning that it was still a countryside of landowners and tenant farmers. It was too undramatic perhaps for fancy housing estates or second homes, and seemed altogether sensible and well-arranged. It looked as though nothing awful, nothing nonsensical or unexpected had ever

COUMEENOOLE BAY, COUNTY KERRY

MWEELREA MOUNTAINS FROM RENVYLE PENINSULA,
COUNTY GALWAY

happened there. The seasons must always have passed, one might think, benevolently from one to the next, while the crops ripened and were harvested, the cows were milked, the country houses elegantly aged, the dry-stone walls disintegrated and were reconstructed, the Nallys exchanged one model of Mitsubishi for the next, and the hum of the tractor, the twitter of the skylark, the caw of the rook linked the generations in sweet threnody.

But, even as I thought these thoughts, I knew what rubbish they were. The Pinnacle, being a lumpish object of blackish crumbling stone, certainly pretended to no revelatory powers, and I was preposterously misreading that countryside. In fact if there is any constancy to Ireland – the westernmost and most pungently individualistic part of all Europe – it seems to me the constancy of perpetual unfulfilment. This is the very kingdom of uncertainty, and far from maturing smoothly down the centuries, the landscape I surveyed had experienced incessant jolts of history. Wild chieftains had fought for its possession, conquering armies had trampled it, famine had ravaged it, alien mountebanks had seized it, religions had grappled for its loyalties, poets, jesters, minstrels, story-tellers, mendicant saints, revolutionaries and vagabond seers had infused it with merriment, malice, holiness, wit, vivacity, skulduggery, superstition and evasion. Ireland might look fine, frank and even obvious, but really I knew very well that it was a prospect of deception, full of secrets and surprise.

Perhaps there was a time when Ireland was relatively straightforward, but it was certainly ages ago, when the world itself was less obfuscated. Prehistorically the island was at least autonomous, out there in the western ocean, populated only by misty neolithics of one supposed sort

BENBANE HEAD, COUNTY ANTRIM

BLACK LAKE, GAP OF DUNLOE, COUNTY KERRY

or another. In the Bronze and Iron Ages it was taken over, if we are to believe the epics, by tribal Celts of grandiloquent temper – chariot-riding, poetry-spouting, curly-bearded – who built themselves tremendous mound-tombs, told each other towering stories, fought Homeric battles and were ruled by mighty kings. Even in historic times the Irish, though split into scores of petty kingdoms, remained more truly themselves than most Europeans, because the Romans never ventured across the Irish Sea, and Christianity, which reached the island in the fifth century, apparently did not much alter the nature of its society. Irishmen spoke the Gaelic language still, founding one of the oldest literary traditions in Europe; Irish tribes maintained their identity; Irish kings governed their ancient provinces; Irish saints, mystics and monks, adding a lovely Celtic gloss to Christianity, not only gave learning and spirituality to their own country, but were the greatest missionaries of the age. It is true that the Vikings, having repeatedly raided the island, established powerful colonies here and there, but still in 1005 the most celebrated of all the Gaelic kings, Brian Boru, was able to proclaim himself Imperator Scottorum – Emperor of the Irish.

But then everything changed. In 1167 the Norman conquerors of England arrived in Ireland too, and from that day to this the history of the island has been variously disrupted, devastated and inhibited by the interference of England. It dominates Ireland's story, especially in the crude historical shorthand of hilltop essayists. By the end of the thirteenth century the English had established a fairly precarious presence in many parts of the island, setting up their headquarters in the former Viking settlement of Dublin and evolving their own landowning class – the Catholic Old English, who presently became as Irish as the Irish themselves. By the end of the sixteenth century they had declared

MAGHERA STRAND, COUNTY DONEGAL

their own Kingdom of Ireland, with its Established Protestant Church of Ireland, and with large areas of land occupied by Protestant immigrants. By the end of the next century the intervention of William III, William of Orange, had sealed the supremacy of the Protestant minority. By the end of the eighteenth century Ireland was officially part of Great Britain, controlled on the spot by a Protestant Ascendancy of landowners, businessmen and clergy; its Catholics were denied all rights, its native aristocracy was mostly in exile, its Irish language overshadowed and its north-eastern province of Ulster largely populated by imported Scottish Presbyterians, led by the contumaciously sectarian Orange Order. By the end of the nineteenth century the island, decimated by the terrible potato famine of the 1840s but appeased, the English hoped, by land reform and the emancipation of the Catholics, lay apparently impotent as a mere appendage of England.

Through it all, however, a sporadic resistance had been maintained, sometimes sullen, sometimes savage, and fired by a perplexing variety of patriots. There were champions of the old order, feudal chieftains of the O'Neills or the O'Donnells, the hunchback Earl of Desmond, Red Hugh O'Donnell of Tyrone. There were Old English patricians, who fought a bitter war against Oliver Cromwell himself in defence of the Catholic faith and the royalist ideology. There were charismatic Protestants such as Wolfe Tone, whose name was to enter the national pantheon. The inspired Catholic Daniel O'Connell, 'The Liberator', revived the idea of patriotism among the common people. For a time it seemed that Charles Stewart Parnell, an elegant Anglican landowner, would achieve Home Rule for Ireland, until the discovery of an illicit love affair cruelly ruined him.

And in 1916 the martyrs of the Easter Rising in Dublin, some

THE BURREN, COUNTY CLARE

Catholic, some Protestant, brought it all to a head, presenting the British with the starkest of dilemmas; though the Catholic majorities of Connacht, Leinster and Munster wanted Home Rule, the Protestant moiety of Ulster wanted continued union with Britain. London responded by separating six of the nine Ulster counties from the rest, creating a self-governing Ireland in the south and west, a Protestant-dominated British province of Northern Ireland in the north-east. The Irish characteristically fought a war among themselves to decide how best to greet the decision, but by the middle of the twentieth century the Ireland of today had come into being: the Republic of Eire, capital Dublin, with 3.5 million people (95 per cent of them Catholics); the United Kingdom Province of Northern Ireland, capital Belfast, with 1.5 million people (28 per cent of them Catholics).

Yet even now nothing is settled. Eight centuries after the arrival of the first Anglo-Norman knights upon the soil of County Waterford, a British army in Northern Ireland is engaged in enforcing the order of the island, separating those who still wish to unite the whole of it under the Irish tricolour from those who are still determined to keep their part of Ulster under the Union Jack. To the mere aesthetic discomfort of partition, which makes the island feel restless and incomplete, is added a rumble of bitterness and violence, to keep the Irish destiny now, as it always has been, sadly unresolved.

So there is really nothing, let alone a stone column on a hill in County Westmeath, that I could genuinely identify as a symbolical fulcrum for Ireland – the Pinnacle itself, I noted, was erected in 1763, at a time when the subjection of the Irish was almost utter, and was all too likely the inspiration of some rapacious Anglo-Irish landlord who was altogether

THE BOG OF ALLEN, COUNTY KILDARE

CRUIT ISLAND, COUNTY DONEGAL

alien to the Nallys of his day. Sitting up there in meditation would provide me with no pattern; irony, ambiguity, mystery, exception were all around me, as I looked out across those misleading meadows. I resolved then that my essay would not after all aspire to paradigmatize Ireland, but would be a roundabout, personal, easy-going thing, more like the country itself.

I touched the Pinnacle for luck anyway, without going so far as to embrace it, and when I scrambled back over the wall I noticed that the boulders I dislodged in crossing, scraping each other as they fell, gave out a queerly sulphurous smell – which might after all have offered me an allegorical opening, if only I could think of it.

I stood one evening on a very different hill, the Rock of Cashel in Tipperary, capped with its tall thicket of ruins – where Brian Boru held court as High King of Ireland, where archbishops dispensed theology and the renegade Earl of Inchiquin, 'The Burner O'Brien', came slaughtering and profaning through the sacred precincts. I stood on this commanding place one summer evening and, looking down to the fields below, observed a black mare with her foal. There were cattle about too, munching and lolloping, and through them those two equines, mother and son, picked their way with fastidious grace. They seemed to me more than animals; the poor cows would eventually be slaughtered, but the mare and her foal looked timeless, as though they would be sauntering always there through the lush grass, in the soft of the evening, beneath the towers of Cashel.

If the Pinnacle of Glassan had failed me, these creatures did exemplify for me some spirit of the island itself. It was a legitimate fancy. In the worst days of English oppression the very name of Ireland was transmuted into a series of exquisite eponyms, presenting the country as a flower, an animal or most often as a lovely girl – Dark Rosaleen, Cathleen ni Houlihan, My Little Dark Rose. The convention survived, and in modern times too artists have habitually portrayed Ireland in metaphor. 'Did you see an old woman going down the road?' asked one character of another in a play by Yeats, resuscitating one of the oldest of these fantasies. 'I did not; but I saw a young girl, and she had the walk of a queen,' says the other – and everyone knew that he was speaking of Ireland.

So I could be forgiven for seeing Ireland in those lovely horses. Recognizable always in this country, it seems to me, are elemental essences – suggestions of fire, love, ethereal beauty, superstition, battle

GLENGARRIFF, COUNTY CORK

BRANDON BAY, NEAR STRADBALLY, COUNTY KERRY

and death. 'I loved the young men whose horses galloped over many an open plain, beating lightning from the ground,' says an old woman in a Gaelic poem, and she too was allegorizing the country, which has always boasted of its hell-for-leather young bloods, and always loved its horses. When they erected a memorial to the dead of the Easter Rising, within the Dublin General Post Office which was the focus of the rebellion, they chose a figure of the mythical hero Cuchulain, who had himself lashed to a rock rather than submit to his enemies – and whose bronze legs in the Post Office are now shining from the touch of so many respectful customers.

The Irish language was always the messenger of these emotions, and it remains today a kind of *memento vitae* – a reminder of Ireland's Celtic origins, and of its immemorial sovereignty. Irish – by then, as the poet Thomas Kettle put it, 'the secret scripture of the poor' – was the symbolical language of the patriots who finally achieved independence from England, and it remains the first language of the Irish State. The Republic of Ireland is officially Poblacht na hÉireann, the President of Ireland is Uachtarán na hÉireann, the Prime Minister is the Taoiseach, the Parliament the Oireachtas. Street signs and official announcements are generally in Irish and in English, in theory Government servants are bilingual, and every Irish schoolchild learns at least a smattering of Irish.

It is a proud but wishful formality – hardly more. The Irish language, passionately revived in the first years of independence, never did become popular, and today it is spoken as a first language only in the areas officially designated as Gaeltacht or Gaelic areas. A visit to one of these enclaves is a haunting experience, especially perhaps for a Welsh

KERRY COAST

MAAMTURK MOUNTAINS, COUNTY GALWAY

KERRY COAST

wanderer. Disregard the effluvia of tourism, never mind the sometimes silly manifestations of Celticness that other Irishmen like to mock – to stand on a rocky shore in Kerry, say, on the ultimate edge of western Europe, and to hear hanging on the air the cadences of that infinitely ancient and lyrical tongue, echoing from a farm door perhaps, or shouted over the beat of rock music from a café, is to sense the deepest power and poignancy of Ireland. Who can doubt that it was Irish that my mare spoke to her colt, as she led him through the meadows of Cashel?

Most of the Gaeltacht areas are in the extreme west, where you would expect them to be – the language was inevitably driven westward by the encroaching English; it has survived most strongly in less urbanized and less fertile parts, and anyway the wild Atlantic landscape seems to suit it best. One, however, I was astonished to find occupying a few square miles on the seashore of County Waterford, in an area otherwise entirely Anglicized and pursuing a kind of agriculture, of dairy farming and mixed tillage, not usually associated with Irish Gaels. This is an odd phenomenon indeed. An Rinn seemed to me like a capsule of another society, deposited, as by unidentified flying object, off the Cork to Wexford road. Its Gaelicness began with its town sign, the Irish above the English, and ended just as abruptly four or five miles on, but in between all was separate and different from the countryside around; street signs, shop signs, conversations, the very air itself, I fancifully thought – the whole place suggested to me a total immersion course in Irishness, as I drove through it bemused.

They say there is a revival of interest in the language, but cynics still scoff at the official preservation of Irish. It can never die, though; for one thing its literature is with us for ever, and for another it has

CARAGH LAKE, COUNTY KERRY

inexpungibly affected the way the Irish think, and the way they speak and write English. The Romans never Romanized Ireland, the Reformation never reformed it, the Industrial Revolution never revolutionized it, the world wars never convulsed it, the British Empire never finally suppressed it, and through all its history the potencies of the language, its myths and its poetry, have kept Ireland intimately in touch with its own origins.

Irish artists have always been under the spell of the language – even Dean Swift, they say, learnt some of his satire from Irish examples – and have repeatedly returned to it, as to the source of their inspiration. The Irish literary renaissance of the 1890s, though it expressed itself in the English of Yeats, Synge and Lady Gregory, founded its lyricism upon the music and vision of the old language. The tragically gifted Brendan Behan, the archetypal stage Irishman, who spent half his life showing off in obscene English in the pubs of Dublin, London and New York, learnt the Irish language, wrote frequently in it, and repeatedly returned to the farthest west for what I take to have been a scouring of the sensibilities. It was James Joyce's Dubliner Stephen Dedalus who said that for an Irishman the English language must always be 'an acquired speech . . . so familiar and so foreign'.

The echo of the Irish language, if not the language itself, has helped to preserve Ireland's links with the pre-industrial world, and almost anywhere in the island I seem to feel myself closer to the pastoral society that has been destroyed almost everywhere else in Europe. Its images are ubiquitous still in the countryside – donkeys, horses, haystacks, black curraghs on the Connemara shore, a couple of goats shackled together in a field, horses, tinker caravans in shambled laager, fusty corner shops, pubs with signs saying 'Musicians Welcome', an old

KENMARE, COUNTY KERRY

LOUGH CONN, COUNTY MAYO

NEAR KYLEMORE, COUNTY GALWAY

woman leading a cow, grinning imp-like children – and a flavour of esoteric whimsy often reaches us still out of the peasant past. Sídheán an Gháire, the Fairy Mound of Laughter, is the name of a tumulus near the Ballymote golf course, in Sligo. A caged billy-goat, beribboned and rosetted high above the market-place, is the king of the annual Puck Fair at Killorglin, in County Kerry. My favourite laugh in Ireland is the laugh I got from the Musical Bridge at Bellacorick, in County Mayo. The rain was pouring furiously when I arrived at this celebrated folk-site, but the Musical Bridge was unaffected. Conveniently to hand a playing stone awaited me and, huddling my jerkin around me, I stepped from the car and slid this small boulder along the wet parapet. Fairy tones, dulcet tones miraculously emanated from the structure, and the faster I ran across that bridge, sliding my stone with me, the more melodious and magical became the music. Headlong through the puddles I exuberantly dashed, and the music bounded with me, and the rain poured, and the passing cars hooted in hilarious applause as they too soaked me with their splashes. There was an old curse on the bridge, they say – the man who laid its last coping stone would inevitably die, and sure enough, hardly had he laid it than he collapsed and kicked the bucket. Nowadays, though, no malediction hangs about Bellacorick's bridge – only a comically merry blessing.

'Musicians Welcome.' The harp of the wandering minstrel is the official emblem of the Irish Republic, appearing on all its coins, besides being the universally known trade-mark of Guinness, the brewers. Nothing is truer to the old spirit than Irish traditional music, which has lately enjoyed a dramatic revival, establishing a cult following all over the world, and which expresses itself most characteristically in pubs. All over Ireland there are taverns known to musicians (and some, like the ones at Doolin in County Clare, have become so famous as to be insufferable, at least during the tourist season). To walk into one sufficiently late on a summer evening can be a startling experience – like coming face to face with a medieval minstrelsy. Solemn in a corner of the bar four or five musicians will be playing some immemorial jiggety air, on tin whistle, guitar, fiddle and drum. The music is flighty, rhythmic, insistent and intoxicating, like the music of fiddlers in fairy tales; the musicians, thumping their feet to its rhythm, are bent over their instruments altogether seriously, almost reverently in fact. Jammed suffocatingly all around them, beer in hand, the young crowd watches and listens as though bewitched, and standing on top of the bar, so as to be seen across their heads, the bar-tender too looks as though he has been magicked there. When the tune ends the players, breaking into satisfied smiles, and exchanging brisk words of badinage with their audience, drink deep of Guinnesses; and very often one sees young foreigners, Germans perhaps, or Scandinavians, staring at them as though they are seeing ghosts.

This defiance of time has seduced many an Irish artist – as Yeats wrote, in a kind of dream:

> *I will arise and go now, and go to Innisfree,*
> *And a small cabin build there, of clay and wattles made:*
> *Nine bean-rows will I have there, a hive for the honey-bee,*
> *And live alone in the bee-loud glade . . .*

It would be naive to call the instinct innocence, or even simplicity. It is more a kind of organic resolution. To my mind it makes Ireland, even now, a more *real* country than most, its towns and cities less false or modish, its countryside more frankly rural. Except for its northern areas of dispute the country remains wonderfully relaxed. Its population is no greater now than it was at the beginning of the eighteenth century, and most of its countrysides are, like the one around Glassan, tranquil and uncluttered. Intensive farming has come to Ireland, and frequently pollutes rivers, but for the most part you would not guess it, so naturally fecund do the fields appear, so languidly do the streams flow, so rich are the hedges and coppices still. In the far west the mountains remain, in their washed light off the Atlantic, like the settings of myth – bare bony hills, sea-shores foam-flecked, cliff-hung and ringed with magnificent sands for the horses of legend to gallop along. Even in the interior of the island, and on the gentle eastern coastlands, perfectly ordinary rural places often seem to me peculiarly euphoric, radiating a kind of complacent glow, or indefinably joyous, so that I expect to find gypsies dancing at crossroads, or revellers reeling home in song.

Sometimes indeed I do, for this is not all literary hyperbole. There cannot be much difference between the faery musicians of legend and the buskers who frequent the streets of Ireland now, between the story-tellers of the heroic past and the raconteurs weaving their fantasies in Irish pubs – striking the same chords, give or take a notation, employing the same anecdotal techniques, if one allows for shifts in the style of exaggeration.

The odd thing is that no country in Europe, except perhaps Spain, has been so drastically modernized in the past twenty years or so. Since the brief economic boom of the 1970s, when Ireland joined the European Community, all the standard contemporary apparatus has fallen upon Ireland – chain store and soap opera, theme park and silage pit, yuppie

THE BURREN, COUNTY CLARE

and unisex hairdresser. Almost a clean sweep has been made of the traditional country cottage, especially in the west; instead, wherever you look there are spanking new single-storey houses, with car-port and TV aerial (most of the houses taken, I understand, from a book of plans called *Bungalow Bliss*, whose author, Mr Jack Fitzsimons, has thereby altered the face of Ireland at least as thoroughly as Wren once transformed London). Tourism, which has long held in its grasp places like Blarney and the Killarney Lakes, has by now reached its dread finger into every last Irish peninsula. In Dingle, which I remember as the remotest of fishing villages, I recently ate *nouvelle cuisine* monkfish washed down with a very palatable California Chardonnay. Dozens of tourist boats a day, together with several aircraft, converge throughout the summer upon the islands of Aran; their passengers are conveyed around the sights in interminable convoys of traps and jaunting-carts, and even as I write I learn of a grandiose plan for 'leisure developments' on the islands, to include that *sine qua non* of tourist fulfilment, a golf course.

Yet still, one feels, beyond the eighteenth hole, this side of the marina, the bean-row flourishes and the glade is bee-loud. Even the towns and cities of the island still feel countrified to me, with their colourful variety of small shop-fronts, like so many village stores. None of the towns is large enough for their centres to be out of sight of the country: Cork, Derry, Dublin, even Belfast, the first industrial city of Ireland, all are still really country towns. In Dublin horses and carts perambulate the streets, and in its principal shopping thoroughfare, Grafton Street, the fashionable store of Brown Thomas still announces itself as General Drapers. In Cork irrepressible gangs hook salmon from the city centre bridges, selling their catches, like poachers in a play, with

GARNISH BAY, COUNTY CORK

NEAR LETTERFRACK, COUNTY GALWAY

DINGLE BAY, COUNTY KERRY

eyes open for the Gardai at nearby street corners. In the poorest and toughest parts of Belfast, Catholic or Protestant, I find only sympathetic responses, as one might expect from rural people. Ireland's urban population indeed is wonderfully quick and eager, as though still revelling in its freedom from all the old country burdens of climate, boredom and mucky labour – like people realizing life's variety for the first time, and paradoxically feeling as I myself feel when, coming from some fumous and preoccupied metropolis, I discover the salt brilliance of the sea.

In Dublin, sitting on a flight of steps near Leinster House, a well-known lady enigmatically lives her life out, day after day, watching the passing world. I pay my respects to her whenever I am there, and she always ends our discourse with the same quaint valediction: 'Cheeryby!' I think of her as archetypal to the city, because although it is the most urbane place in Ireland, a national capital and a city of international celebrity, it seems to me the most elemental of them all – I nearly said the most guileless, until I remembered the threads of evasion, intrigue and rivalry, frequently curdling into malice, which notoriously run through every aspect of Dublin life. Contemporary Dublin often suggests to me a city of the Third World, shambled and decrepit, plastered all over with advertising signs, degraded with hideous new buildings, smelling nowadays less of Guinness than of hamburgers or fried chicken, dangerous in its less reputable quarters but nevertheless full of life, fun, vigour, music and youth.

It is still, as it famously always has been, the city of the instant response, charged with a shot of irreverent humour. I once called the Dáil to ask if there was anything interesting to be seen there at the national assembly that evening: 'There's always me,' replied the duty usher, 'I'm interesting.' I went to a party recently at the National Gallery which ended with three elderly and distinguished gentlemen singing a song of their Omagh childhood sonorously and hilariously down the lofty corridors and through the columned portico: 'It was written by my brother-in-law,' one of them confided to me in passing, as if to explain everything, 'he used to be a great footballer and is still alive, I'm glad to say, though of a vast age.'

I cannot begin to count the number of instant acquaintances I have struck up over the years at Bewley's Oriental Café in Westmoreland Street, where the shyest of casual visitors, once she has settled to her strong tea and rich sticky bun, and seized the occasion to comment upon the weather to the party at the next table, need not be lonely for long. The pubs of Dublin, too, which are not only the delight of the populace but also the pride of the Tourist Board, live up to their reputation for easy hospitality to young and old – a late reflection, I like to suppose, of the classic Celtic tradition which afforded any stranger on the roads food, wine and shelter. The policemen of Dublin at least know how to turn a blind eye: 'I'll have a word with the garda' is a familiar and reassuring promise of this capital. The innumerable musicians of the Dublin streets are like the harpers and minstrels of the past, and the beggars who haunt the city bring to its very centre a pungent suggestion of the nomadic. One night I walked out of the Gaiety Theatre, after a performance of Brendan Behan's *Borstal Boy*, into the sudden explosion of lights, stir and laughter that succeeds a happy evening at the theatre, especially after a play every line of which the audience seems to know by heart – I emerged into all this fizz to find on the sidewalk immediately outside a dark-skinned, long-skirted, barefoot woman holding her baby to her breast and her hand out for alms; she was a

THE TWELVE PINS, CONNEMARA, COUNTY GALWAY

touching sight indeed, but she seemed to me, I have to say, a perfectly proper part of the scene, quite compatible with the merry and loquacious theatre-goers now strolling away through the night lights for a pint or two at Davy Byrne's or O'Donoghue's.

And if you think the Dublin face of the old cartoons has disappeared from life – the bucolic boxer's face, I mean, bulbous and rubicund, which used to represent to the world the spirit of backstreet Ireland, generally equipped with a knobkerrie stick, a speckled scarf and a battered stove-pipe hat – if you think it has vanished, try visiting the Four Courts on any sessions day, when, beyond the buzz of the massed bewigged legal profession in the lobby, a stunning assembly of Paddies, ould wans and wide-boys still awaits the call to justice.

Once the most elderly in western Europe, the population of Ireland is now the youngest, and inevitably there are signs of its absorption into the rest of Western culture. The influence of television, rock music (Ireland is very strong on rock – Sham-rock they call it), materialism and general trendiness is as apparent here as anywhere else, and I imagine that the wilfully deracinated Irishman, speaking a flattened Euro-English and looking for his example to Brussels, New York or London, is going to be more and more common as the years pass. But for the most part Irish people, at most levels of society, remain powerfully indigenous of temperament. The general image of the Irishman, I fear, has him ribaldly comical at a bar, engaged in violence of some kind, or singing sentimental ballads in a maudlin tenor: a truer stereotype, if one could scrape away the deposits of opportunism and historical pressure, would be a figure far more sensitive and calculating.

Calculating, because there is of necessity in the Irish character an

BALLYNESS BAY, COUNTY DONEGAL

element of wariness. There has had to be, to see this people through the hazards of history. Boozers and brawlers, however entertaining, do not see to it that a nation survives. A sharp eye for self-defence, an articulate wit, a somewhat fatalistic faith in one God or another, cunning, a basic kindliness, ready laughter and a not infrequent streak of the malevolent – these seem to me the generic qualities of Irishness, which give this island its atavistic strength. They are contagious qualities. If the Scottish settlers of the north-east have not all acquired them, retaining to this day an indigenous stern stubbornness, all too often the English immigrants of the Catholic south developed all the Irish characteristics, from the tendency to strife to the reckless generosity of attitude so often interpreted by foreigners as fecklessness.

So far as I can see the Irish have relatively little regard for worldly consequence, beyond the universal aspiration of keeping up with the O'Briens. They can take it or leave it, and the Republic's institutions of State are resolutely lacking in pretension: I went to the installation of a new President once, and throughout the ceremony in the Great Hall of Dublin Castle, attended by most of the leading men and women of the Republic, a celebrated Irish actor kept his neighbours in a state of improper hilarity with his murmured running commentary. There are many places in Ireland which claim association with eminent Americans – Ulster alone claims to have nurtured eleven Presidential families – but they generally treat the fact casually enough. Ballyporeen in County Tipperary, where the Reagans came from, does indeed have a Visitors' Centre, but the most memorable token of the connection is a hugely blown-up photograph in O'Farrell's pub, captioned 'President Reagan during his visit here on 3rd June 1984 drinking a pint of Smithwick's, Ireland's No. 1 Ale'. At Dergalt, in County Derry, a cousin of President Wilson showed me round the Wilson homestead; but while he looked remarkably like his famous relative, without the pince-nez, and told me that his own nephew Woodrow worked on a nearby farm, he was far more eager to talk about the Northern Ireland troubles, which he thought could easily be settled by a determined dictator, than about the Treaty of Versailles. And Ms Mary Ann Ryan, who was working in the yard when I arrived at the ancestral farm of the Kennedys, at Dunganstown in County Wexford, admitted to being a cousin of J. F. K. but seemed to think it nothing very remarkable; there is a little museum in the last fragment of the original homestead, with pictures of visits by the President and his brother Bobby, but the sign announcing the presence of the place to passers-by is overgrown with creeper – 'I suppose we ought to clear it really,' said Ms Ryan amiably, but without conviction.

No nation honours its great writers more loyally than the Irish, but they are remembered less in graves and memorials than in the scenes they celebrated or the taverns they enjoyed. I was not in the least surprised, entering the Greville Arms hotel in Mullingar one day, to find James Joyce apparently at work on a new novel in a telephone box behind the reception desk; he was a waxwork actually, in a glass case, but looked absolutely at home opposite the lounge where, as it happened, an especially knees-up kind of disco dance was taking place that evening, enjoyed by many a grand old lady indulgent over her pint of stout on the sidelines. The most touching literary memorial I know is the ruined rectory at Lissoy in County Westmeath, where Oliver Goldsmith grew up; now no more than a shell filled with jumbled farm implements, plastic bags and odd piles of building equipment, it most appositely honours his genius – for as Thackeray said, one cannot think of Goldsmith without a pang of pity. On the other hand, I arrived one day at Drumcliffe Church in Sligo, where Yeats is buried beneath his

own celebrated epitaph ('Cast a cold eye/On life, on death./Horseman, pass by!') to find a large congregation assembling for the annual Yeats Day service, attended by devotees from many parts of the world, including the Co-Convenor of the Yeats Society of Western Australia, and graced by the unmistakably Yeatsian presence of the poet's son Michael.

To my eye this is an almost classless society, give or take a few earls of course. Very few Irishmen, even the most urbanely and cosmopolitanly educated, lose all trace of a brogue; at a dinner table one evening I sat next to a particularly worldly gentleman farmer, Oxford-educated, Royal Navy-bred and with connections in the City of London, and it was fascinating to observe how steadily, as the conversation warmed and the differences of opinion agreeably deepened, the old Irishness of his intonation came to the surface. Besides, in a population not only on the whole the best-looking in Europe, but also among the most intelligent, I can seldom tell from citizens' faces (except perhaps in courtrooms) whether they have been expensively nurtured or have come up from the bogs.

In short, the Irish remain very Irish. They remain true to their beginnings, and proper to their setting. Green, after all, is not only the overwhelming colour of the Irish countryside, but the national colour of the Irish Republic (though in fact St Patrick's blue was the traditional colour – it turned to green when they mixed it with the Protestant orange of the north). The Irish are generally as amused as anyone else by the Irish joke, which presents them as comically stupid and boorish; their lingering old-fashionedness seems to me sophistication of a paradoxically modern kind, subtly sustaining their affinities, as nowadays we would all wish to, with nature, legend, the land and the past.

GLEN OF AHERLOW, COUNTY TIPPERARY

3 A PROPENSITY TO FAITH

Ireland has always been holy. Even the climate of the place, a disturbed alternation of clarity and blur, seems made for mysticism, and in my experience the profound simplicity that I have been trying to elucidate opens the way to speculation and conviction. I am more contemplative in Ireland than almost anywhere else.

Consider this family of Irish people, sitting beneath a canopy in the drizzle of a Marian shrine near Cappoquin in County Waterford. The image of the Virgin is not very old, but it stands sufficiently arcanely on a rock wall in a frond-filled grotto, with a stream running below. Though immediately beside a country road, the place is always half in shadow, and during the past few months the statue has repeatedly been seen to move of its own accord, and to be transfigured. Sometimes its face changes into that of Christ, and sometimes it apparently comes to life – only last night, a bright-eyed lady at the gate tells me, she met the Virgin walking silently by the stream (she met Jesus there once, too). Every day pilgrims come to this small rural shrine, and by its entrance now the group of women arranging candles, plastic bags and artificial flowers reminds me irresistibly of the busy old ladies who surround holy shrines in Hong Kong.

However, I have never seen Chinese in the religious condition of the family beneath the canopy. They sit there, mother, father, adult son and daughter, in a determined common trance, their eyes fixed immovably upon the statue on the rock – willing it to move, praying for a manifestation, clutching rosaries, lips moving sometimes but bodies stiff as images themselves.

The Irish propensity to faith, some would say to credulity, obviously pre-dates the arrival of St Patrick with the news of Christianity. The

INISHEER, ARAN ISLANDS

LOUGH CORRIB FROM DERREENMEAL, COUNTY GALWAY

entire island is strewn with magic totems far older than that – if not older physically, certainly older spiritually – and it could be said indeed that the devotion of the people at the Cappoquin shrine pre-dates the divinity they worship. Cromlechs of uncertain significance stand on many an Irish hill, stone circles arise in bleak and boggy moors, and in every part of the island there are sacred sites to whose shrubs and trees people have undoubtedly been tying their shreds of cloth, their torn handkerchiefs and their discarded shirts since the days of paganism. Here and there are clumps or patches of particular holiness, like the clusters of tombs or sacred stones on the islands of Lough Erne, or the scattered necropolis of Brugh na Bóinne, in County Meath. There you may stand on the great passage tomb of Dowth, once crowned with a tea-house, now brooding beneath its tangle of brambles, and look across fields littered with tumuli and standing stones to the mysterious mound of Newgrange, Si an Bhrú, into whose central chamber, on the day of the winter solstice every year for several thousand years, the dawn sun has sacramentally fallen.

As a pantheist myself, I love those Irish places where Christianity long ago absorbed the pieties of paganism. It gave me an eerie frisson, for example, to sit in the sombre chair of St Kieran in St Canice's Cathedral, Kilkenny, in which the Bishops of Ossory are enthroned, because it is credited with supernatural powers far beyond the episcopal jurisdiction. It stirred me in a primitive way to wander around the peculiar pilgrim site of Glencolumbkille, in Donegal, because its fifteen stations are a *mélange* of the heathen and the Christian – piles of pebbles, a circle of stones, a roofless chapel, cairns, cross-slabs, a megalithic tomb. I was moved to think that the summer festival at the holy well of St Brigid, near Lahinch, is really a late observance of Lughnasa, a festival dedicated to the god Lugh which was one of the great events of the ancient Celtic calendar. The well is approached through a whitewashed grotto-like tunnel, cluttered with holy pictures, crudely scrawled prayers, discarded crutches and ex-votos of all kinds, but for centuries a magic eel was supposed to live in it, and at Lughnasa the people of the Aran Islands came over in their currach flotillas to revere its mysteries and give thanks to the great old god.

In Faughart in County Louth there is a shrine dedicated to St Brigid which incorporates a modernistic glass-enclosed altar and a statue of the saint, but which is centred frankly enough upon a collection of prehistoric healing stones, each labelled with its anatomical reference – the eye stone, the foot stone, the waist stone, the knee stone with deep knee-shaped grooves in it, the head stone against which, since I was suffering from migraine when I visited the place, I duly knelt to rest my head. Among the great sights of Ireland is the Janus stone of Boa Island, in County Fermanagh: casually among the nettles in a neglected cemetery stand two stone imps or deities, back to back, goggle-eyed, cross-belted, wide-mouthed, bearded or pointed of chin, who look as though they have been standing there, shoulder to shoulder, head to head, since the beginnings of belief.

All the power of pagan fear and dedication, then, added muscle to the Christian faith, and helped to strengthen the sanctity of Ireland. As all the world knows there are Protestants in this island. There is the tiny minority of Protestants within the Republic, perhaps 100,000 of them, their churches often charmingly faded or crumbled, their epitaphs wonderfully nostalgic; there is the powerful majority of Protestants in Northern Ireland, perhaps 750,000 of them, dominated by Scottish-

SKIBBEREEN, COUNTY CORK

descended Presbyterians of formidable tenacity. Some 3,600,000 Catholics, though, set the spiritual tone of the island as a whole. The Irish Republic is, in effect, a Roman Catholic State. The Catholic hierarchy may no longer be all-powerful in matters of public morality, but is influential still: at least 80 per cent of the Republic's citizens still go to Mass on Sundays, and if not as many find vocations nowadays in holy orders (there are far fewer priests and nuns about), nevertheless when there was a referendum recently to decide whether divorce should be legalized in the Republic, by two to one the people voted the Church's way. Faith still dictates the style and the aspiration of republican Ireland, if only subliminally. At six in the evening on Irish State television everything pauses for the sounding of the Angelus, accompanied by a sacred picture on screen, and nothing is more genuinely Irish than one of the island's still frequent manifestations of religious fervour.

The peripatetic Virgin of Cappoquin was only one of many which excited the entire nation in the 1980s. The frenzy began one night in July 1985, when several people visiting a wayside shrine to the Virgin at Ballinspittle, County Cork, seemed to see the holy statue swaying in the half-light. Drawn to the site by their tale, hundreds more people reported similar experiences. The Press got hold of the story, rumours flew around the island, and in no time at all holy statues all over the Republic were on the move, frequently sponsoring holy apparitions too, and sometimes delivering messages of suitably hierarchical import (advising citizens, for instance, how to vote in the divorce referendum). Sundry scientific explanations were offered, mostly concerned with mass hallucination; sundry priestly comments were published, generally concerned with the miraculous and inexplicable love of God; the English travel writer Eric Newby went to Ballinspittle itself, where at

CLEW BAY, COUNTY MAYO

NEPHIN BEG RANGE, COUNTY MAYO

the height of the excitement a daily average of 5,000 people expectantly watched the statue, and to his surprise did see it move, 'not just backwards and forwards, but from side to side'. From Wexford to Donegal, as evening fell each day, devout multitudes gazed longingly at images of the Virgin, as steadfast in their hope as my spellbound family in the Cappoquin drizzle.

Statues still move now and again, though when I went to Ballinspittle myself I found the miraculous shrine a little run-down. Californian fundamentalists had knocked the head off the figure ('and if it moves again we'll be back'), and though it had been repaired some of the thrill seemed to have left the place. The tiered benches, which had once held thousands of silent watchers, were empty in the evening, and only a solitary man was praying before the famous figure when I dropped by. But in any case the grand momentum of Catholicism swings on regardless of such cyclical enthusiasms, and expresses itself more majestically in the four great permanent pilgrimages of Ireland, which are anything but transient crazes, and which draw their multitudes as regularly and as inexorably as the seasons themselves.

The most theatrical of the four destinations is the shrine on the summit of Croagh Patrick, a mountain in County Mayo upon which St Patrick is supposed to have spent forty days and forty nights in AD 441. Pilgrims climb the 2,500-foot peak every day of the year, but on the last Sunday of July hundreds of people ascend it, preferably before dawn and without shoes, to worship at a windy and rubbish-strewn oratory at the top. I once stood near the foot of the climb on a day of ferocious storm, hoping for literary purposes that some suitably striking devotees, a party of elderly shoeless nuns, for instance, would emerge out of the

NEAR OWENREAGH RIVER, COUNTY KERRY

CAHA MOUNTAINS, COUNTY CORK

MICHAEL KING, COUNTY GALWAY

mists radiant from their experience; in the event nobody emerged at all, but even so I felt, as I peered aghast through the driving rain and howling wind towards the cloud-swirled summit, before returning limply to the car and making for the nearest café – even so I felt for myself, weakling that I was, some of the harsh magnetism of the mountain (which is known familiarly as The Reek, and has gold in it, actually, as all holy hills must).

The most charming pilgrimage site is a place near Rosslare, in County Wexford, called in Irish Cluain na mBan, the Meadow of the Women, but Catholicized as Our Lady's Island. This is the very model of a civilized sacred place. A small village with a steepled church, some of its houses whitewashed or thatched, looks down upon a small grassy peninsula in a salt lagoon, separated from the sea by a sandbar. It has been a place of pilgrimage certainly for 500 years and probably for much longer. Besides the statutorily ugly glass-roofed altar, and the usual white effigies of the Virgin (one of them, the faceless one now, as it happens, fashioned by a local craftsman using no tools but a spoon) – besides these conventional equipments there are the ruins of an Augustinian priory, a toppled castle keep and an overgrown graveyard. Around the perimeter of the twelve-acre spit, fresh when I was there with buttercups, cowslips, daisies and clover, squawked and flapped over by gulls, rooks and herons, the devotees on pilgrimage days progress in their hundreds by an idyllic grassy path. In the old days they used to do it on their knees, sometimes half-immersed in the sedgy water of the lake; nowadays as they make the holy circuit, telling their rosaries, a sequence of loudspeakers encourages them on their way with prayers and hymns.

The most robust and booming place of pilgrimage is undoubtedly

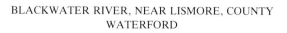

BLACKWATER RIVER, NEAR LISMORE, COUNTY
WATERFORD

Knock, in County Mayo. Here in 1879 the Virgin Mary made the most celebrated of her Irish appearances, illuminated together with St Joseph and St John the Evangelist upon the gable wall of the village church. Hundreds of thousands of people come to Knock from all over the world – it is the Lourdes of Ireland, with many miraculous cures recorded, and when Pope John Paul II visited the village in 1979 it was said that the rest of Ireland would merely be a side-trip for the Pontiff. A massive off-modernist basilica now dominates the place, big enough to hold 20,000 worshippers, and a glass atrium encloses the gable wall itself, long picked clean of all its cement by seekers of sacred relics. There are car parks everywhere, and hotels, and souvenir shops, and fast food restaurants, and all the energies of twentieth-century mass pilgrimage. More in the original spirit of the place, though, is the narrow passage behind the shrine, up which people squeeze one after the other to kiss an unenticing brown spot upon the wall – the nearest available place to the actual site of the apparition. Thanks to the efforts of a dynamically entrepreneurial pastor, the late Monsignor James Horan, Knock now has its own international airport, twelve miles out in the empty hills, big enough to accept Jumbo-loads of the devout, and also offering regular tourist services from London, Paris, Brussels and Amsterdam. When I was in the sanctified village the burning issue of the day was whether or not to allow more car rental companies to set up shop within the airport precincts: as is said in one of the innumerable pamphlets about the village, whose miracle was for many years doubted by the Catholic hierarchy, 'Knock has evidently stood the test of time.'

But for my pagan tastes the most compellingly holy of all these holy destinations is St Patrick's Purgatory, on an island in Lough Derg in

BENBANE HEAD, COUNTY ANTRIM

MWEELREA MOUNTAINS (NEAR DOO LOUGH), COUNTY MAYO

County Donegal. I was once at a wedding reception at Drogheda, away on the east coast, when I heard a beflowered matron, making small talk, ask an executive-type young man with a carnation button-hole where he was planning to go for his holiday that year. I expected Barbados or Crete, but no. 'I thought of giving myself,' he said, 'the three days at Lough Derg.'

Anyone in Catholic Ireland would know what he was talking about, and it seems that few would be surprised. Making the pilgrimage to Lough Derg is rather like going to a health farm, in some more effete society, or perhaps going to the National Eisteddfod in Wales. The reputation of the place was not always so benign. Lough Derg is a forbidding lake (there used to be a monster in it), the landscape around is desolate, and when St Patrick found his way there he experienced in an island cave a vision of the pains of purgatory, that way-house between heaven and hell. It was to re-enact his testing torments that the pilgrimage was instituted, probably in the twelfth century, and we are told that it powerfully impressed the purgatorial doctrine upon the popular mind. Today's penitential pilgrimage is certainly not easy, but at least the conclusion is foregone; survive three days at Lough Derg, and you are a step nearer heaven.

Modern pilgrims are ferried out to Station Island in spankingly maintained, but very old-school, motor-boats, like naval picket boats. A sombre complex of buildings awaits them, domed and cloistered, filling the entire island and reminding me of those institutional islets, hospitals, prisons or lunatic asylums, which used to dishearten the Venetian lagoon. The pilgrims undertake to spend three days and two nights out there, with only tea, dry bread and hard buns to sustain them. They spend one entire night in vigil, and nine times in the course of their

WILLIAM O'NEILL, CAHIRCIVEEN, COUNTY KERRY

ONE-MAN BAND, BALLINASLOE, COUNTY GALWAY

MOURNE MOUNTAINS, COUNTY DOWN

stay they must process barefoot, rain or shine, around a series of stony 'beds' (actually the remains of medieval monkly cells) reciting Christian mantras at each – in all, sixty-three Glorias, 234 Creeds, 891 Our Fathers and 1,458 Hail Marys. It is a fearfully demanding penance, yet every year it is undertaken eagerly, joyously even, by thousands of housewives, farmers, schoolteachers, physicians, students, lawyers, writers, businessmen and yuppies straight from weddings. It is, it seems, an intensely personal self-trial – as Seamus Heaney wrote in a poem about the pilgrimage, 'a road you travel on your own'.

I spent an hour one day on the neighbouring shore (one can visit the island, during the pilgrimage season, only as a pilgrim), contemplating not so much the somewhat drear prospect as the astonishing fact of the pilgrimage. Seven or eight hundred people were on the island at that moment, I was told by the car park attendant, who had made the pilgrimage twenty-one times herself, and through my binoculars I could see that the place teemed with life, like an ant-heap in the water. Scores of people sat or walked upon the quayside, sometimes I caught the flicker of a surplice, and in gaps between the buildings I could see pilgrims endlessly queuing to perform their rites at one or another of the stations – St Patrick's Bed, perhaps, or St Brigid's Cross. Not a sound reached me across the water, not even a bell or a priestly chant: the island seemed utterly insulated, as though enclosed within a transparent screen, and the strange incessant movement of the people seemed in my fancy to make the whole place eerily heave and stir.

Presently three buses arrived from Dublin, and from them clambered the day's quota of new pilgrims, all with their raincoats and their hold-alls. They looked less like holy palmers than patients anticipating a short stay in hospital. Some looked distinctly apprehensive, as though

BEN BULBEN, COUNTY SLIGO

they were in for short sharp surgery, some happily expectant, as though for the maternity ward, and some could not help wearing the expression of benevolent condescension that marks, in all such situations, one who has done it before. All, though, seemed to me to exhibit in their bearing a strength of purpose, a resolution of character, that most of us summon only at moments of crisis or tragedy. They were off to their barefoot, hungry, sleepless ordeal altogether voluntarily. I do not know the contemporary theological rationale behind the pilgrimage to Lough Derg, but as a challenge to the human spirit before the event, as a satisfaction of achievement afterwards, I can easily accept its truly purgatorial power.

GORUMNA ISLAND, COUNTY GALWAY

4 THE HEROIC MODE

One of the holiest places of all is Clonmacnoise, the Meadow of the Son of Naois, in County Offaly. It is a glorious monastic settlement on a wide bend of the Shannon, but when I went there one July evening I thought it more militant than spiritual. A windswept compound of chapels, graves and shrines, with the remains of a cathedral, a round tower and a magnificent high cross, it looks out across the wide river to bare fen country, marshy and deserted. Far away one can see the buildings of Athlone, whence in 1552 came a waterborne English army to sack the sacred establishments. In the hazed summer dusk I almost thought I could see the armoured men in their boats terrifyingly rowing down the wide curves of the river towards me, while the monks and priests manned their tower and bolted their gates. I did not find Clonmacnoise very sacred of numen, but I thought it in its shattered defiance a place of true epic.

Many another old Irish building gives me the same excitement. The great spiky castle of Dunluce is one; Thackeray thought it looked 'dragon-guarded', on its cliff above the sea in County Antrim, and although it is no more than a gaunt wreck, howled through by the sea-winds, it still looks to me as though some wizard-king might be in residence. The lake-fortress called The Bawan, hidden away in Lough Doon in County Donegal, is thrilling in a still more sinister way, for it is a great stone ring rising out of the water with a baleful grandeur, far from human habitation, surrounded by dismal moorlands and entered only through a single door. As for the Grianán of Ailech, the circular sun-palace of the Kings of Ulster, it seems to command half of Ireland from its hilltop in Donegal, ringing always with vanished arms, ablaze with invisible flags – a place where a king could truly feel a king. The old Irish certainly knew how to build splendidly, and so they should, for

ACHILL ISLAND, COUNTY MAYO

PURPLE MOUNTAIN, COUNTY KERRY

among the varied elements of this island's character, shining through the strange, the sad, the homely and the malevolent, the heroic is seldom absent.

Irish legends are full of heroes far larger than life, far braver, more generous, more demanding and more handsome, and sonorous names, titles and phrases resound through the annals – the Knights of the Red Branch, the Red Hand of Ulster, Niall of the Nine Hostages, the Hag of Beara, the Pirate Sea-Queen of the West. Rhodomontade, too, has always been endemic to Irish art, especially to that quintessential Irish art, inherited direct from the craft of the story-tellers, the art of conversation. Oh, what majestic fellows, what marvellous women, parade through a good Irish anecdote, whether it be a reminiscence in a saloon bar or a snatch of a great novel! In the face of the heroic, especially perhaps the tragic heroic, Irish sensibilities seem to flower and Irish reason is suspended. Most of the great figures of Irish history apear to me heroic in their various kinds: miraculously heroic like legendary champions, violently heroic like Grace O'Malley the Pirate Queen, satirically heroic like Dean Swift, flamboyantly heroic like Oscar Wilde or Brendan Behan, fatedly heroic like the martyrs of the Easter Rising, romantically heroic like Yeats, Parnell or that majestic and indomitable patriot, Maude Gonne.

For myself I can easily be stirred, often against my better judgement, by the memorials of English imperialism in Ireland, the myriad castles and mansions and churches and follies and obelisks which speak of an old conquest and an almost lost culture. At one extreme, the blood-curdling, there is the horrific memorial at Lisburn, County Antrim, to that furious revenger of the Indian Mutiny, John Nicholson, who was seen at the time as the very exemplar of an Anglo-Irish soldier; he is portrayed at Lisburn in the act of decapitating, or perhaps disembowelling, a fortunately invisible victim, sabre raised maniacally above his head; there is a memorial to him in the neighbouring cathedral, too, which adequately describes him as 'the type of the conquering race'. At another extreme, the magisterial perhaps, there is the grave Anglo-Norman fortress of Cahir in County Tipperary, which presides with dragon weathervane over its modest country town; the lovely River Suir forms its moat, with a row of Georgian houses clustered courtier-like on the bank, while at the weir men with big forks rake the river for weeds, and skinny youths swim and frolic. Somewhere in the middle stands what is left of the Dublin the English built. With its fine Georgian squares, its graceful bridges over the Liffey, the elegance of Trinity College and the splendid space of O'Connell Street (*né* Sackville, after the Lord Lieutenant of the day), it is neither arrogant nor paternalistic, but speaks of a gentlemanly confidence, and reminds me, now that it is overlaid, defaced and mucked about with shoddiness, of many another ex-British city similarly treading away the vestiges of Empire.

The Anglo-Irish as a whole were, if nothing else, a people of style. They devised many a thing of Irish beauty, whether it be a country house or the layout of a market town, and among foreigners indeed their social attitudes – dashing, reckless, assured, ironic – were interpreted for a couple of centuries as the classic Irish manner. 'Tall, strong, handsome chaps' Friedrich Engels thought them in 1856, with 'enormous moustaches under colossal Roman noses', and if the indigenous Irish frequently resented their presence, detested their postures and burnt down their mansions when the chance arose, there is no doubting that they envied these colourful imperialists their self-assurance.

BLASKET ISLANDS, COUNTY KERRY

The surviving Anglo-Irish have inevitably gone down in the world since the Irish Republic gained its independence. No longer are they the masters of the countryside as of the hunt, the dictators of style, the pastors of affluent Sunday populations. I had mixed feeings at Killala, in County Mayo, once an Anglican diocesan city, on finding its cathedral shabby and shuttered, its bishop's palace gone and its consequence now provided by a Japanese synthetic fibre factory on the hill behind. I have never much liked the sound of Lord Kitchener, but I did see a poignancy to his birthplace, Gunsborough Villa in County Kerry, once a trim Anglo-Irish shooting lodge, now a less than spanking farmstead up a rutted lane. At the foot of the hill of Tara, coronation seat of the High Kings of Ireland and one of the great symbols of Irish national consciousness, a particularly Anglican church stands with its church-yard, full of exceptionally Anglican monuments, actually protruding into the storied site. Hearing one day that there was to be a great Church of Ireland festival there, attended by Anglicans from far and wide, I made my way to Tara hoping for a good assortment of those handsome big-nosed fellows and their ladies: but the all-confident style had gone, there were no lean freckled patricians in tweeds, and the congregation on its benches outside the church, though accompanied indeed by a brass band and addressed by a vicar in full canonicals, seemed to me more or less indistinguishable from any country assembly of Irish papists.

There are Protestant places in Northern Ireland where one may still catch a little of the old atmosphere. The text-book Plantation town of Hillsborough in County Down, for instance, is where the British Secretary of State for Northern Ireland has his official residence, an eighteenth-century mansion with a fort in its park; the steep main street of this showplace runs away in authentically deferential decorum from

KERRY COAST

SPERRIN MOUNTAINS, COUNTY DERRY

WICKLOW MOUNTAINS, COUNTY WICKLOW

the castle gates and the courthouse, while the parish church of St Malachi (the first Irishman to be canonized) is approached by an avenue of alternate limes and rhododendrons, and has a birdbath in its churchyard in memory of the composer Sir Hamilton Harty. Within the Republic the most allegorical habitation of the Anglo-Irish is probably the pretty village of Castletownshend, in County Cork, where for several generations the Somervilles and the Townshends, two of the best-known Ascendancy families, lived in large houses at opposite ends of the street, carrying on in a wonderfully Anglo-Irish way – writing books, that is, experimenting with photography, sending their sons off to the Royal Navy and frequently intermarrying. When I visited the place in 1970 I actually heard a Townshend hail a Somerville in the village street with the greeting 'Morning, Cousin Robert', and even now the village feels obscurely squirely of style, neater, more ordered, more detached from the soil than any settlement of the native Irish.

Indeed there still are Townshends and Somervilles in Castletownshend, for here and there even in the Republic survivors of the Ascendancy inhabit their country houses – this is one place in the former British Empire where the imperial caste has sometimes hung on to its acquisitions. In their prime these were often wonderful. The now demolished Coole in County Galway – Coole of the Seven Woods – was where the writers of the Irish literary renaissance used to assemble at the turn of the century, where Yeats saw his nine-and-fifty wild swans on the lake, and with its mixture of the wild and the ultra-civilized, its collegiate-like garden and its reedy river, it must have been paradisaical. Fota, in County Cork, now institutionally owned, occupied an entire island of the estuary known as Cork Harbour, filling it from water to water with meadows, gardens and a superb arboretum; it had its own

INISHEER, ARAN ISLANDS

POWERSCOURT, COUNTY WICKLOW

railway station, too, for the exclusive use of the Smith-Barry family. At Powerscourt, now a ruin in the Wicklow Mountains, one of the most famous gardens in Europe airily embraced the shapely Sugar Loaf Mountain within its plan. Belvedere House near Mullingar, in County Westmeath, municipal property now, not only had the loveliest walled garden imaginable, but was graced by a peculiarly lavish Anglo-Irish folly: a mock castle wall, with battlements and arrow-slits, erected by the first Earl of Belvedere to blot out the view of the next-door house, in which his wife had once enjoyed a surreptitious affair with his own brother.

The remaining imperial families generally live more modestly, in reduced but still thoroughbred circumstances, exemplified by scuffed stair-carpets, generous portions of supermarket sherry, ancestral portraits largely disregarded, numberless prints of historical scenes or imperial episodes, old copies of *Burke's Landed Gentry*, bent ha-ha railings and lawns precariously kept in trim amidst the encroaching wilderness of the demesne. I find these circumstances beguiling, and I confess that sometimes I am retrospectively seduced by the sheer bravado of the English presence. What fun they must have had! What incomparable prizes they won! In County Waterford I once drove into the thickly timbered demesne of Curraghmore, in the rich river country east of the Comeragh mountains. It was like driving through an untamed forest, the road twisting and turning, the only sign of life an occasional cottage deep in the woods, until I came suddenly upon a wide glade. In this stood the house of the Marquis of Waterford, fronted by an elegant forecourt that reminded me of a French parade ground, with clipped chestnuts that looked like orange trees. The house was an ungainly affair, crowned by the heraldic figure of St Hubert's stag, its

WHITE PARK BAY, COUNTY ANTRIM

cross standing between antlers which were, I later learnt, real ones. There was no sign of life. The place seemed entranced. Only the trees sighed a little in the wind, and the hills stood blue-grey and silent beyond. Never have I have been so envious, as I stood there under a spell myself, of conquest's inherited privilege.

There is a dark and distorted heroism to the endless struggle of the Irish guerrillas, Republican or Unionist, fighting their murderous secret campaigns in the north. Their causes may be misguided, their methods often despicable, some of them are doubtless no more than thugs, opportunists or even psychopaths, but at least some are courageously staunch in their ideals.

Rather to my dismay I found Belfast, the embattled metropolis of their conflict, the most truly mettlesome of all Irish towns. Its stance is naturally grand, immediately between the mountains and the sea, and so is its light, which is keenly, rather severely brilliant, without the soft lambent charm of the south and west. Its origins are also robust, for it was born out of that tremendous age in which the British married ideology to technique, and made industry a tool of Empire. The city is equipped with all the idioms of Victorianism, a monumental City Hall, wide business streets, huge cranes above shipbuilding yards, and the Linen Hall Library, which is a very temple of self-help. No urban scene in Ireland, for my tastes, is more impressive than the view down Royal Street, along Donegal Street, past a pinnacle building which ought to be something monumental but is really the former premises of Robinson and Cleaver the drapers, to the towering mass of City Hall; this is a behemoth of imperial assertion, domed, turreted, surrounded by *fin de siècle* plinthed worthies, flying the Union Jack of course and plastered

LUGNAQUILLIA MOUNTAIN, COUNTY WICKLOW

ASHLEAM BAY, COUNTY MAYO

THE CLIFFS OF MOHER, COUNTY CLARE

with a huge and characteristic slogan: BELFAST SAYS NO.

What the city is municipally rejecting, some years after the event, is the 1985 agreement between Britain and the Republic, which allowed Dublin a vestigial say in the governance of Northern Ireland. The Unionist response to this initiative was an almost unanimous thumbs down, but the slogan on the City Hall seems to me a symptom not only of this particular refusal, but of the city's inflexible devotion to its several causes. There are, of course, thousands of Belfastians who only want a quiet life and reconciliation, but the flavour of the place is set by the dogmatic resolution of its implacable Unionists on the one side, its irrepressible Republicans on the other.

After so many years of conflict some parts of Belfast look like war zones, yet there is a terrific spirit to the city. It is an astonishingly resilient place. I am told that for all the hideous tensions, the kangaroo courts, the sectarian killings, the knee-cappings and the constant harassment, Belfast's general state of mental health is no worse than any other city's. South of the river, where the Protestant Orangemen have their strongholds beneath the shipyard gantries of Harland and Wolff, huge showy graffiti decorate the houses, flaunting heady slogans like CROWN AND FLAG FOR EVER, embellished with florid painted images of King William of Orange and his white charger. North of the river, in the Catholic enclaves, the tricolour of the Republic predominates, and there are scrawled encouragements to the IRA – OUR TIME WILL COME, with pictures of masked gunmen and automatic rifles. The relentless and somewhat childish ebullience of it all very soon palls, masking as it does such ugly emotions of resentment and revenge, but I could not help admiring, somewhat shamefacedly, the sheer bloody-mindedness of the place.

There is a street corner in Ballymurphy, one of the most uncontrollably Republican districts of north Belfast, which on the right day flaunts its contempt for law and establishment with great panache. It is a block of shops and offices which looks at first sight like some kind of fortress, windows blocked, doors barred, walls scarred, the whole indefinably congealed in dirt and dispute, but bursting with vigour. In the streets outside half a dozen London taxis are carelessly parked – vehicles of the Black Taxi system, originally a Republican paramilitary service, now semi-legally public. Around the corner a couple of lawyers boldly announce their premises, and are expert no doubt in cases of civil disturbance or infringement of the Anti-Terrorism Act. Twos and threes of formidable young men hang here and there about the place, posters and slogans are everywhere, and over it all flag upon Republican flag flutters in the breeze. When I was there it was indeed more than a breeze, but a mighty wind off the mountain, and the violent gusting of it, the slap and crack of the flags, the grim but dynamic nature of the block, the suggestive force of those young men, combined that day to give the Ballymurphy street corner a touch of epic excitement.

One more glimpse of the heroic mode in action: the Prentice Boys' march in Derry (Londonderry to the Protestants), annually commemorating, under the auspices of the Orange Order, the successful defence of the city against the Catholic siege in 1689. This gave me one of the most extraordinary experiences of my life, when I attended its 300th celebration in 1989. Never did I see such a variety of remarkable faces, pinched, florid, genial or fierce beneath their bowler hats and tam-o'-shanters – the most truly Irish of all faces, I was tempted to think. Never were pipe-and-drum bands more fervent or exhibitionist. Never was I in a crowd so absolutely united in its enthusiasm. Thirty thousand

DUN AENGUS, INISHMORE, ARAN ISLANDS

THE GIANT'S CAUSEWAY, COUNTY ANTRIM

DENNIS HEGARTY, BALLINASLOE, COUNTY GALWAY

Orangemen took part in the march, and for five hours an air of perfervid dedication enveloped the city. There were tiny boys of three or four marching with the rest. There were half-crazed bass drummers and clown-like drum-majors, juggling their batons, balancing them on the ends of their noses, strutting and gesturing like circus performers. There were ranks of stern elderly men, bowler-hatted, some carrying swords, all swathed in the regalia of the Orange Order. Halfway down the procession the hero of the Ulster Protestants, the Rev. Ian Paisley, came swaggering by with a cohort of aides, smiling here and there and cheered all along the way like a dictator moving among his adoring subjects.

Armoured trucks and camouflaged soldiers stood by, and in the course of the morning an IRA bomb went off, but the momentum of the festival was irresistible anyway. Hour after hour it continued, and the beat of the drums reverberated, and when I left Derry the Orangemen were still streaming across the Craigavon Bridge, banners flying, drummers prancing, determined old men in bowler hats in steadfast line abreast. They really would die, I think, before they handed over Londonderry to the Catholics, whose quarter of the city, Bogside, lay silent and watchful on the hill above.

These are partisan heroics, like most heroics, I suppose. There is, however, a more profound nobility to Ireland, which springs from the nature of the place itself, its islandness, its antiquity and its perseverance. It is registered constantly in images: awful cliffs of the western shore, swans and herons on lonely lakes, the wild fuchsia of the Irish summer, soda bread and foaming stout, the grand rivers, the immense black bogs, haunting mountains, like Ben Bulben in County Sligo or

Slieve Gullion in Armagh, the fantastic rock-monastery of Skellig Michael away in the raging seas, the grey karst mass of the Burren ('not enough wood to hang a man with, not enough soil to bury him'). I stayed once in a hotel in Cork near the River Lee, and during the night a thick fog came out of the ocean and fell upon the city, masking everything in a greyish-yellow light; all night long I could hear echoing through this mist the generators of a German warship lying at the quay below, with guttural commands over loudspeakers half-muffled by the vaporous mass, and I felt as I lay and listened how utterly insular Ireland was, there among its mists and winds, with the ships in its harbours all round.

Grand! Grandness itself, grandness epitomized is the Herculean fortress called Dun Aengus on Inishmore, the largest of the Aran Islands. Clip-clop, oy!, hup, hup! your jaunting-car takes you out there from the landing-stage, out through the stony landscape, past ancient tombs beside the road, with the coast of Connemara bright beyond the sound and the gulls whirling over the rocks. Your driver greets his friends in the Irish language, as he has for several thousand years, and whenever you look are the mazy stone walls that he and his forebears have erected over the millennia. An old woman takes flowers into a church. Three black curraghs lie on a foreshore. Hup, hup! grunts the driver when we come to a hill, and the horse responds for a brief moment as if to humour him.

So you come to Dun Aengus on its cliff-edge. Its great semi-circle of stone walls ends vertiginously on the very rim of the cliff, dropping away a couple of hundred feet to the sea below. It is like a fortress erected not against human enemies, but against the forces of destiny itself. It faces nothing but empty sea for 3,000 miles, and behind its back all Ireland seems to brace itself, like Cuchulain on his rock.

WHITE PARK BAY, COUNTY ANTRIM

5 'YOU HAVE STILL GOT A DARLINT PLAN'

Even over that spectacular place a hint of sadness loiters. Melancholy is endemic to Ireland. The fragility of the climate is part of it – the sunshine so palely brilliant but so ephemeral, the feeling that the weather is never set, but may shift in mood from one hour to another. The landscape, too, can be poignant, especially in the rain. The boglands then seem an earnest of the final desolation, and when the boughs are dripping even a leafy country lane in Ireland can feel awfully forlorn. They say that Dublin itself has its dispirited moments, when the wittiest repartee somehow falls flat, and everyone goes home early.

But undoubtedly the *tristesse* of the island is chiefly man-made, climate and terrain being only accessories. Of all national histories, Ireland's must be one of the saddest – a perpetual quest for serenity, conducted amid sporadic bloodshed, heartbreak and recrimination for seven centuries and more. The old struggle is generally identified today by that peculiarly Irish euphemism, 'The Troubles', and its mementoes span the ages. If Clonmacnoise was sacked by the English in 1522, many a gaunt ruined house was burnt by the Irish in the 1920s; Cashel of the Kings has been crumbling into decay for 300 years, but in the towns of Northern Ireland you may come across ruins created by bomb-blast or arson only the other day. At Wexford in the south-east they remember the rebels of 1798, slaughtered and thrown into the River Slaney; at Mullaghmore in the west they remember Lord Mountbatten, assassinated in his boat in the harbour in 1979.

Today the prime symbol of The Troubles is the border between the Republic and Northern Ireland, imposed in 1920 from County Down to County Derry, and at one point reaching almost to the western coast – County Donegal is connected with the rest of the Republic only by a

BLACKROCK, COUNTY LOUTH

CLEW BAY, COUNTY MAYO

CLEW BAY, COUNTY MAYO

ten-mile corridor. It fractures the ancient province of Ulster, a final reminder of the destruction, down the centuries, of all the Irish kingdoms. More miserably still, it perpetuates the fundamental tragedy of modern Irish history, the intrusion into this island's affairs by that great and terrible neighbour, England.

Spending a few days wandering along the border is a chill and sometimes eerie sensation. It is strange enough to find oneself coming out of the Poblacht na hÉireann – where the Uachtarán ceremonially presides and Dáil Éireann legislates, where the tricolour flies and the postal vans are green – into a province where the Union Jack flies and the postal vans are red, the law is decreed (for the autonomy of Northern Ireland was suspended in 1974) by the Houses of Lords and Commons far away in Westminster, and the Head of State is the Queen of England. The people north of the border may seem just the same as those south of it, at least in Catholic villages, but their circumstances are dramatically different.

It is a very queer border, some of its frontier points heavily manned by soldiers and customs men, some entirely open. I asked a woman in Clones, County Monaghan, why some crossings were marked on my map with flags: 'That's the places,' she said, 'you're not allowed to smuggle things through.' An unmistakable aura of skulduggery hangs over it. There is an incessant coming and going of cars along country lanes, buying cheap no doubt, selling dear, taking advantage of all those fiddles and chances that flourish along international frontiers every-where. At the chief border posts long lines of trucks await their customs clearance on their way south to Dublin or Galway, north to Belfast or Derry; but at scores of entrances a more shadowy traffic flits and scuttles across unimpeded.

The sadness hits you when, having entered Northern Ireland unchecked by one of these convenient back-doors, a few miles up the road you are stopped by a British Army road-block. It is likely to be a faceless thing of concrete and sandbags, masking the road in front rather as a spirit wall masks the garden of a Chinese house, but when a traffic light summons you inside its barricades you find yourself accosted by two young soldiers, helmeted and heavily camouflaged, one pointing an automatic rifle directly at you, the other shouting the number of your car to an unseen comrade within the guard-post. A few impassive questions, an inspection of the car, and you are waved on: it is courteous enough, in a mechanical way, but it leaves you as you continue your journey with a sense of revulsion – that those unsmiling figures from over the sea, so utterly alien to all things Irish, should through history's injustice be in command of that gentle Armagh lane. Jim McAllister, a Republican poet of the border, has written that if he were ever to die in the hands of the British Army there, at least he would be at home in his own land; but to the soldiers his place of death would be no more than 'map reference 13, Sheet 3, South Armagh . . .'

The British are no longer present as occupiers, only as reluctant peace-keepers, and I imagine that hardly a trooper among them would not rather be out of the cursed island for good. But this makes the sensations of the border only the more pitiful. The racial and religious hostilities of history have long since been complicated by other antagonisms (nationalists v. loyalists, guerrillas v. the forces of the law, radicals v. conservatives, Royalists v. Republicans). Asking the way to the shrine of St Brigid at Faughart, itself only a mile or two north of the frontier, I was told to turn left at a pub called the Three Steps. It sounded a jolly direction, and I considered stopping off for a drink and a

ATLANTIC OCEAN FROM CARRIGAN HEAD, COUNTY DONEGAL

sandwich, until I remembered with a pang why the name sounded familiar – it was in the car park of the Three Steps, not so long before, that a British undercover agent had been kidnapped by guerrillas, his body never to be seen again.

Ever and again in this haunted country one comes across monuments to the dead, of one side or the other: here ten Protestants gunned down by the IRA at Kingsmills in County Armagh, remembered now in gold lettering on black shiny marble; there three young Catholics ambushed and killed by British undercover agents at Strabane in County Tyrone, commemorated by three wooden crosses in the field where they died. In the churchyard at Scotstown, in County Monaghan, I stood before the grave of Seamus McElwain, a young IRA man whose whole life had been a succession of bloodshed and imprisonments, until he was killed by British soldiers in a nearby meadow. His epitaph was in Irish, and on the cross, together with the relief of a bird escaping through a mesh of barbed wire, was affixed a coloured photograph of him, a good-looking dark-haired boy in a dinner jacket. The tears came to my eyes as I stood there (the wind rustling the hedges all around), and a gardener working nearby asked me if perhaps I was a McElwain myself? But I said I was simply crying for them all, whatever side they were on. 'That's the truth of it,' he said, 'that's the truth.'

In some places the fact of the contemporary Troubles is so much a part of life that the people continue their daily affairs apparently oblivious to the bizarre and awful things happening all around them. In Belfast hardly anybody seems to notice the weirdly screened and armoured trucks that trundle around the city, or the infantry patrols that wander ever and again down perfectly ordinary city streets – I saw a patrolling soldier one evening, in Donegal Square which is the very

heart of Belfast, tuck his gun under his arm for a moment in order to draw some money out of a cash-card machine. In the country many villages seem able to close their eyes to the army installations hideously embedded in their midst, shut off from the community by barbed wire or high walls, their radio aerials protruding high above the rooftops. Eerie tall watchposts stand in the middle of the countryside, and on back-roads along the frontier you may see white crosses painted on the tarmac – location signs for the army helicopters which perpetually prowl around.

The unhappiest place of all seemed to me the village of Crossmaglen, in south Armagh, made notorious over the decades by the many killings and bombings there. It stands in the heart of what the tabloids like to call the Bandit Country, or the Killing Fields, where the Irish Republican nationalists, though within British territory, are in generally unchallenged control, and on my way there I saw a large hand-written notice attached ominously to a telegraph pole, warning that somebody or other was an informer.

I would not like to be that man in Crossmaglen, for the whole village felt privy to conspiracy. It was very silent, very empty, and people seemed to talk to each other generally in undertones. They tell me known Protestants, let alone members of the armed forces, are distinctly unwelcome in the town pubs, and even in the coffee shop where I stopped for a hamburger (having given the Three Steps a miss) people responded to my bright enquiries kindly enough, but warily, avoiding my eye, I thought.

Poor Crossmaglen! A pleasant enough village, like many another, it ought to be a place of convivial merriment, and pehaps one day it will be, but for the moment it is terribly depressing. The large central square

PORT, COUNTY DONEGAL

MACGILLYCUDDY'S REEKS, COUNTY KERRY

BOUGHILL, COUNTY KERRY

(in which at least seventeen British soldiers have been killed) is surveyed from one side by an indescribably sinister army post, thirty or forty feet high, surrounded by barbed wire and made of brownish concrete, through whose narrow slits silent figures, vaguely to be discerned, stare down upon the village – over their gun barrels, one assumes. It is like some monster of space fiction, or perhaps a robot. Immediately below this fort is a memorial erected by the populace to their own patriots, in Irish and in English:

Glory to you all, praised and humble heroes,
who have willingly suffered for your unselfish and passionate love of Irish
  freedom.

I stood in the silence and copied the inscription in my notebook, and when I walked away I saw a hand forlornly waving me goodbye from one of those fortress slits.

Sad in a different way is the sense of emptiness which even now gives the island of Ireland, when the wind is wrong, or the light too grey, a suggestion of abandonment. After the great potato famine of the 1840s nearly a quarter of the Irish population emigrated, and since then a constant haemorrhage of emigrants, mostly young and vigorous, has bled the nation. They still leave in their scores of thousands every year – for England, for Australia, for the United States (where many young Irishmen achieve illegal entry by blarney, by quick wits and by the collusion of relatives). By European standards Ireland is a half-empty island. Even its cities sometimes feel as though they could easily absorb a few thousand more citizens, and large expanses of the countryside are hardly inhabited at all.

SHEILA O'SHEA, SNEEM, COUNTY KERRY

SHEEN RIVER, COUNTY KERRY

All this, of course, helps to sustain the easy ambience of the place, meaning that policemen need not be too officious, that roads are seldom crowded, that people have time to talk. But it is an affliction too. In the west there are empty moors, wild and lonely, which were once farmlands; in the heartland villages sometimes seem to be enduring a perpetual holiday, so empty are their wide streets, so quiet even in the middle of the day. I feel in such a place not only the sorrow of the village, but the homesickness of its children far away.

The chief emigrant port, in the days of mass exodus by sea, was Queenstown, now Cobh in County Cork. From this magnificent haven, also in those days an important base for the British Navy, hundreds of thousands of Irish families set off for Canada and the United States. Their last sight of Ireland, as their ships sailed past the islands to the open sea, was the spired silhouette of St Colman's Cathedral, high on a ridge above the town. With tears, prayers and music they left the green island behind them, and the Atlantic swell bore them off.

Today Cobh is one of the most attractive towns in Ireland. It is built on steep hills above the harbour, with two jolly squares facing the sea, and is all jumbled and cluttered, and full of pubs and ironmongers. A few big ships come and go, there is a constant movement of small boats across the harbour, and high above it all St Colman's still stands in grey protection. But when I went up there one day to think about the place, looking out across the wide bay and its islands (one a well-known penal settlement, one the main base for the half-dozen ships of the Irish Navy), a sense of heartbreak overcame me all the same. The harbour, which had looked so bright and bustling when I walked up the hill, now seemed desolate. The islands lay there loveless. Through the headlands the open sea looked cold, unwelcoming and unending, as though it had

COUMEENOOLE BAY, COUNTY KERRY

DINGLE BAY, COUNTY KERRY

KERRY COAST

no farther shore; and the great church behind my back suddenly seemed to me the image of valediction, forever waving goodbye, regretfully and perhaps reproachfully, to the ships we could no longer see.

I very soon, however, cheered up, when I walked down West View again, it being a street of brightly painted gabled houses jammed together on so precipitous a slope that they looked as though they might at any moment slither all the way down to the sea. West View is enough to cheer up a manic depressive, and in my experience Ireland itself is just the same. If a passing cloud, a hangdog hamlet, an item of news from Crossmaglen, a historical memory or a ruined house can plunge one instantly into melancholy, just as abruptly cheerfulness breaks in. Like the clown of tradition, Ireland is a mixture of merriment and pathos; I like to fancy that those twin figures of Boa Island were meant to express this very aspect of the whole island, for it seems to me that though they both look fairly lugubrious, one does have the vestige of a twinkle in its old stone eye.

Besides, for better or for worse the melancholy is dispersing. Economically modern Ireland has had its exuberant ups, its disappointing downs, but in general things are nothing like as bad as they used to be. Even the miseries of history are receding. If the troubles of Northern Ireland are dispiriting enough on the spot, to the vast majority of the Irish people they seem extremely remote, even irrelevant, and at recent elections in the Republic the question of partition has scarcely been an issue at all. Even in Belfast everyday life proceeds with considerable gaiety, and in most parts of town you are far more likely to be kept awake by pub music, or student high jinks, than by bombs or rifle fire.

In general Ireland is probably happier now than it has ever been, at

DONALD CAMPBELL, DERRYDRUEL, COUNTY DONEGAL

NEAR DUNGLOE, COUNTY DONEGAL

least in historical times. The Republic seems to me, the outsider, a well-run and reasonably efficient small State. It has all the modern services, it enjoys close links with the outside world, and it shares with the rest of western Europe many of the symptoms of consumerism. Who would have expected, only twenty years ago, Ireland's rash of Tudor-style Executive Home Developments? Who would have guessed that Grafton Street would be lined with international chain stores? Who would have dreamt that any Irish magazine would carry, as *In Dublin* carried recently, an advertisement in which a Wicked Bi-Sexual Girl Seeks Attractive Naughty Lady for Mutual Punishment?

At the same time I feel no sense of completeness, of absolution or of relief. Not only does the wound of partition fester still, attended by the ghosts of old emotion, but all that modernism seems less than satisfying. Is this indeed the destiny of the place – to be happy, but never *quite* happy? Is it the very lack of fulfilment, like a fugue never resolving itself, that gives Ireland its inner freedom – as though the human soul itself is not meant to be mapped out logically from a pillar on a hill? To all the Celtic cultures there is a theme of yearning, suggesting that these peoples of the western coasts are constantly looking at once backwards and forwards to a lyric Golden Age, whether it be an age of poetry and romance or an age of universal video. In Ireland the instinct seems to me curiously atrophied or compromised, as if the yearning is for what exists already. If the island could be united in sovereignty at last – if all its economic problems could be solved at a stroke – if not a soul wished to emigrate – if the very climate could be adjusted to provide a perfect constancy of solace – even then, I have the feeling, Ireland would devise other means of unfulfilment.

To be honest, I hope so. In despondent moments I occasionally think

GLENARIFFE, COUNTY ANTRIM

150

THE BURREN, COUNTY CLARE

BEN BULBEN, COUNTY SLIGO

that Ireland is actually becoming much like all other countries. I sense the native wit slackening rather, the native brogue flattened by the examples of television, the Gaeltacht areas retreating ever more shyly into themselves behind the mask of tourism, the Catholic and Protestant certainties subsiding into the usual agnostic apathy, the IRA no more than the reminiscing of tedious old men, the legend, the strangeness and the heroism of things subsumed at last into ordinariness.

But then, almost invariably, some wild quirk of humour or initiative, some glorious anomaly, some arbitrary opinion, some pang of sweet melancholy reassures me, as the houses of West View cheered me up that day. It will be a long time before Ireland is altogether ordinary, and there are times indeed when I think that it is itself the true norm: that all other countries should be aspiring to the fragile Irish balance of content and dissatisfaction. Ireland is still a liberation after all. It is still one in the eye. It remains law and disorder. It is for ever bitter-sweet. One of its most characteristic geniuses, the poet and humorist Brian O'Nolan (alias Flann O'Brien, alias Myles na Gopaleen) wrote a poem eulogizing that great solace and talisman of his nation, a glass of ale – 'a pint of plain' in the vernacular:

When things go wrong and will not come right,
Though you do the best you can,
When life looks black as the hour of night –
A PINT OF PLAIN IS YOUR ONLY MAN.

In time of trouble and lousy strife,
You have still got a darlint plan,
You still can turn to a brighter life –
A PINT OF PLAIN IS YOUR ONLY MAN!

MACGILLYCUDDY'S REEKS, COUNTY KERRY

At similar black and lousy moments I am often tempted to think that IRELAND ITSELF IS YOUR ONLY PLACE.

When I had nearly finished this essay somebody told me that not far from the Pinnacle of Glasson, on an island in Lough Ree, there was a second, rival monument, also claiming to be the geographical centre of Ireland. Perhaps, my informant suggested, I might get more satisfaction there?

But I ignored him.

BENBANE HEAD, COUNTY ANTRIM

CRUIT ISLAND, COUNTY DONEGAL